Newspaper Carriers

by Sandra J. Christian, M.Ed.

Consultant:
William P. Johnson
Director, Circulation Marketing
Newspaper Association of America

Bridgestone Books
an imprint of Capstone Press
Mankato, Minnesota

Bridgestone Books are published by Capstone Press
151 Good Counsel Drive, P.O. Box 669, Mankato, Minnesota 56002
http://www.capstone-press.com

Library of Congress Cataloging-in-Publication Data
Christian, Sandra J.
    Newspaper carriers/by Sandra J. Christian.
    p. cm.—(Community helpers)
    Includes bibliographical references and index.
    ISBN 0-7368-1131-1
    1. Newspaper carriers—Juvenile literature. [1. Newspaper carriers. 2. Occupations.]
I. Title. II. Community helpers (Mankato, Minn.)
HD6247.N5 C48 2002
381′.450713—dc21
                                        2001003339

Summary: A brief introduction to the work newspaper carriers do, the tools they use, the
    people who help them, and their importance to the communities they serve.

Editorial Credits
Megan Schoeneberger, editor; Karen Risch, product planning editor; Linda Clavel,
    cover production designer; Katy Kudela, photo researcher

Photo Credits
Capstone Press/Gary Sundermeyer, cover, 6, 8, 10, 12, 16, 18
DAVID R. FRAZIER Photolibrary, 14
Sandy Christian, 4
Shaffer Photography/James L. Shaffer, 20

1 2 3 4 5 6 07 06 05 04 03 02

Table of Contents

Newspaper Carriers

Newspaper carriers deliver newspapers so people can read the news. They deliver newspapers to houses and apartment buildings. Newspaper carriers also bring newspapers to libraries, schools, and businesses.

What Newspaper Carriers Do

Newspaper carriers deliver newspapers to customers on routes. A route is a path that newspaper carriers follow to deliver newspapers. They place newspapers in newspaper boxes or on steps. They deliver newspapers in the morning, afternoon, or evening.

customer
a person who buys
goods or services

Types of Newspaper Carriers

Walking newspaper carriers walk or ride bicycles to deliver newspapers. Motor route carriers drive cars or trucks to deliver newspapers. Some newspaper carriers have daily routes. Other carriers deliver only on weekends or certain days of the week.

Where Newspaper Carriers Work

Most newspaper carriers work outdoors. Some newspaper carriers deliver newspapers inside apartment buildings or office buildings. Many newspaper carriers work in their own neighborhood. Other carriers must travel to their routes.

Tools Newspaper Carriers Use

Newspaper carriers carry newspapers in a canvas bag. They use rubber bands to roll newspapers. Plastic bags keep newspapers dry. Some newspaper carriers ride bicycles. Others use in-line skates or scooters. Motor route carriers drive cars or trucks.

canvas
a type of strong cloth

What Newspaper Carriers Wear

Newspaper carriers must dress for the weather. They wear t-shirts and shorts when it is warm. They wear a coat when it is cold. They need good shoes for walking. Some newspaper carriers wear clothing that reflects light. This clothing helps people see carriers in the dark.

reflect
to cause something to bounce off a surface

How Newspaper Carriers Learn

A circulation manager teaches new newspaper carriers. Newspaper carriers must know their routes. They learn when and where to deliver the newspapers. They also find out what to do if a customer goes on vacation.

circulation manager

a person who is in charge of newspaper carriers

People Who Help Newspaper Carriers

Bundle drivers bring newspapers to the homes of newspaper carriers. Workers in the newspaper office collect payments from customers. Family members sometimes help newspaper carriers roll or deliver newspapers. Customers can help carriers by leaving a light on outdoors.

How Newspaper Carriers Help Others

People should know what happens in their community. Reading newspapers helps people learn about important events. Newspaper carriers help their customers by delivering newspapers to them.

Hands On: Make a Newspaper

Newspaper publishers create the newspapers that carriers deliver. You can make your own newspaper and deliver it to family and friends.

White paper, 8.5 by 14 inches (21.6 by 35.6 centimeters)
Markers or crayons

1. Fold the paper in half to make pages.
2. Choose a name for your newspaper. Write it across the top of the first page.
3. Draw one picture on the top half of each page of something that has happened in your neighborhood. Maybe your friend hit a home run in a baseball game. Or maybe your neighbor's cat had kittens.
4. Write some sentences below each picture. Tell what is happening in the picture.

You can make extra newspapers to deliver to your family and friends. They will be able to read about what is happening in your neighborhood.

Words to Know

bundle (BUHN-duhl)—several newspapers tied together; bundle drivers bring newspaper bundles to newspaper carriers.

canvas (KAN-vuhss)—a type of strong cloth

customer (KUHSS-tuh-mur)—a person who buys goods or services; newspaper carriers deliver newspapers to customers.

deliver (di-LIV-ur)—to bring something to someone; newspaper carriers deliver newspapers to customers on routes.

publisher (PUHB-lish-er)—someone who makes and sells printed things such as newspapers or books

reflect (ri-FLEKT)—to cause something to bounce off a surface

route (ROUT)—a set path that newspaper carriers follow to deliver newspapers

Read More

Bentley, Nancy, and Donna Guthrie. *The Young Journalist's Book: How to Write and Produce Your Own Newspaper.* Brookfield, Conn.: Millbrook Press, 1998.

Kalman, Bobbie. *Community Helpers from A to Z. AlphaBasiCs.* New York: Crabtree Publishing, 1998.

Internet Sites

Carrier Corner—Safety Tips
http://www.wisinfo.com/carrier/safety.html
Fun Facts About Newspapers
http://216.167.68.146/info/funfacts.html

Index